THE ESSENTIAL COLLE

SCHUMANN

GOLD

Published by:
Chester Music Limited,
8/9 Frith Street, London W1D 3JB, England.

Exclusive Distributors:
Music Sales Limited,
Distribution Centre, Newmarket Road, Bury St Edmunds, Suffolk IP33 3YB, England.
Music Sales Corporation,
257 Park Avenue South, New York, NY10010, United States of America.
Music Sales Pty Limited,
120 Rothschild Avenue, Rosebery, NSW 2018, Australia.

Order No. CH66863
ISBN 1-84449-066-1
This book © Copyright 2003 by Chester Music.

Music engraved by Note-orious Productions Limited.
Compiled by Quentin Thomas.

Printed in the United Kingdom.

Your Guarantee of Quality:
As publishers, we strive to produce every book to the highest commercial standards.
The music has been carefully designed to minimise awkward page turns
and to make playing from it a real pleasure.
Particular care has been given to specifying acid-free, neutral-sized
paper made from pulps which have not been elemental chlorine bleached.
This pulp is from farmed sustainable forests and was produced
with special regard for the environment.
Throughout, the printing and binding have been planned to ensure a sturdy,
attractive publication which should give years of enjoyment.
If your copy fails to meet our high standards, please inform us and we will gladly replace it.

www.musicsales.com

CHESTER MUSIC
part of the Music Sales Group

London/New York/Paris/Sydney/Copenhagen/Berlin/Madrid/Tokyo

The Happy Farmer

from Album For The Young, Op.68

Composed by Robert Schumann

Animato e giocoso

The Reaper's Song

from Album For The Young, Op.68

Composed by Robert Schumann

Little Study

from Album For The Young, Op.68

Composed by Robert Schumann

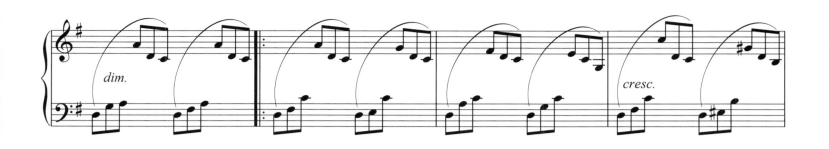

rit.   a tempo

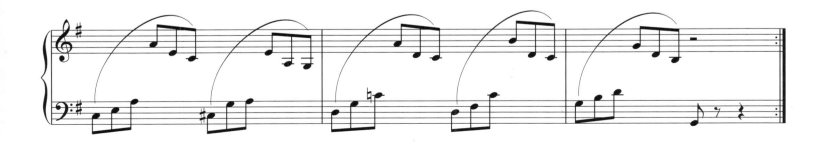

Molto Lento

from Album For The Young, Op.68

Composed by Robert Schumann

The Wild Horseman

from Album For The Young, Op.68

Composed by Robert Schumann

Phantasietanz
(Fantasy Dance)
from Album Leaves, Op.124

Composed by Robert Schumann

Sehr rasch

Lied Ohne Ende
(Song Without End)
from Album Leaves, Op.124

Composed by Robert Schumann

2.   **Leidenschaftlicher**

Tempo I

Romanze
from Album Leaves, Op.124
Composed by Robert Schumann

Chiarina

from Carnaval, Op.9

Composed by Robert Schumann

Passionato

Chopin
from Carnaval, Op.9

Composed by Robert Schumann

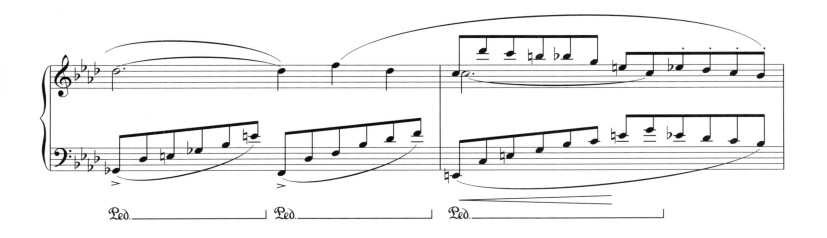

rit.

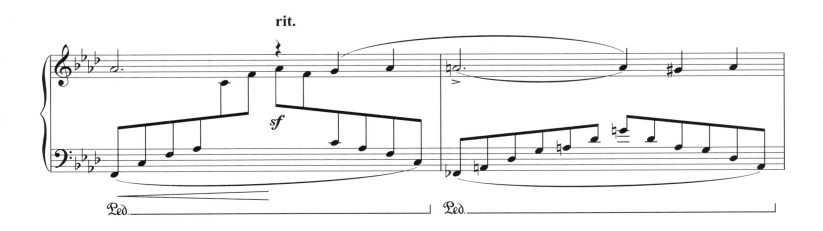

a tempo

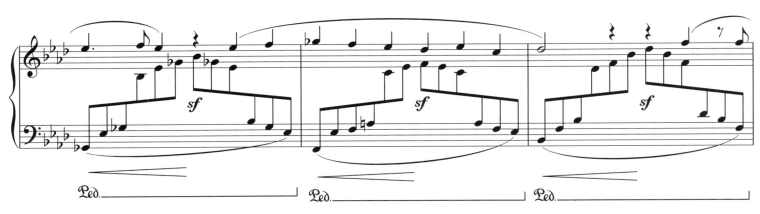

24

March

from Coloured Leaves, Op.99

Composed by Robert Schumann

Molto sostenuto

Trio

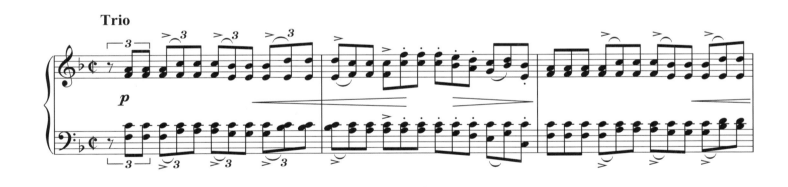

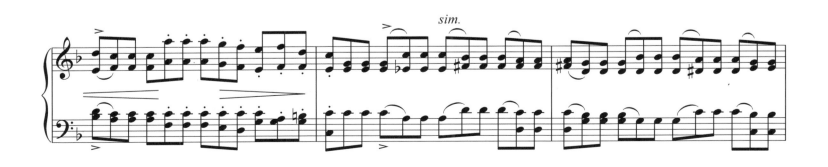

Novellette

from Coloured Leaves, Op.99

Composed by Robert Schumann

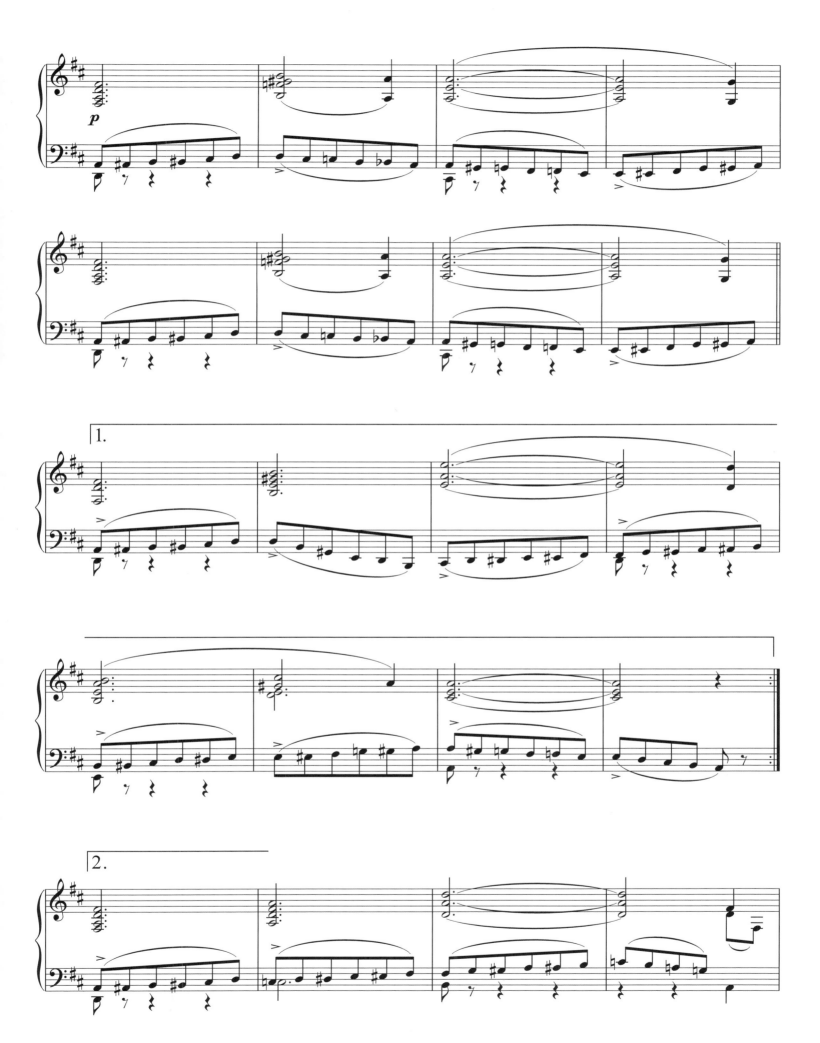

Lebhaft
(Spirited)
from Davidsbündler / 18 Character Pieces, Op.6

Composed by Robert Schumann

rit. Im tempo

Innig
(Heartfelt)
from Davidsbündler / 18 Character Pieces, Op.6

Composed by Robert Schumann

rit.　　　　　　Im tempo

rit.　　　　　　Im tempo

Mit Humor
(With Humour)

from Davidsbündler / 18 Character Pieces, Op.6

Composed by Robert Schumann

Schneller

45

46

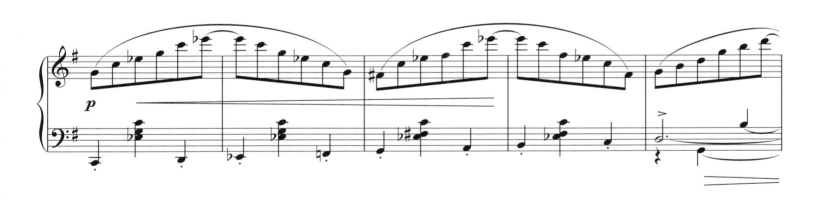

Warum?
(Why?)
from Fantasy Pieces, Op.12

Composed by Robert Schumann

Langsam und zart

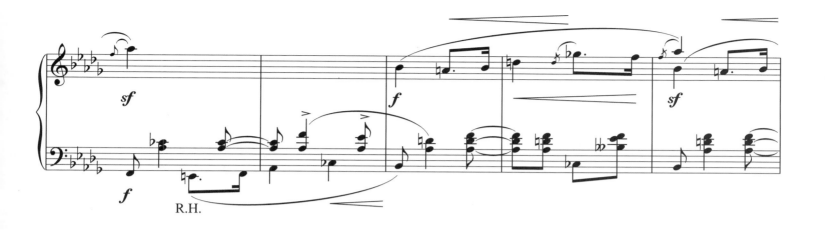

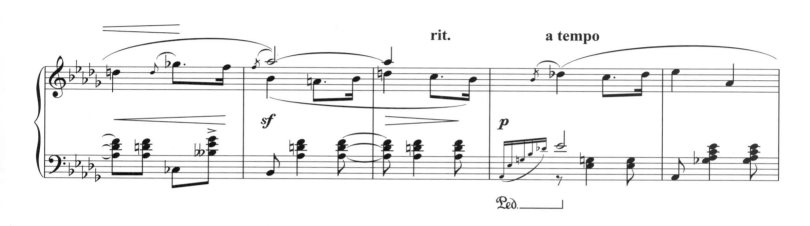

Friendly Landscape
from Forest Scenes, Op.82

Composed by Robert Schumann

Romanze
from Imaginary Pictures, Op.26
Composed by Robert Schumann

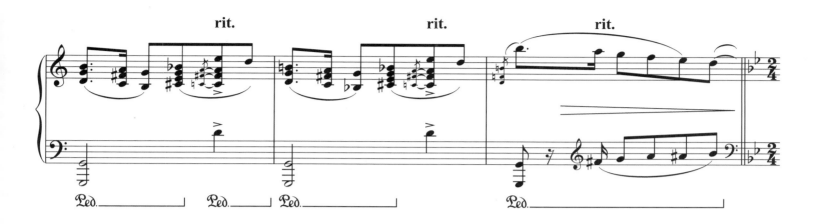

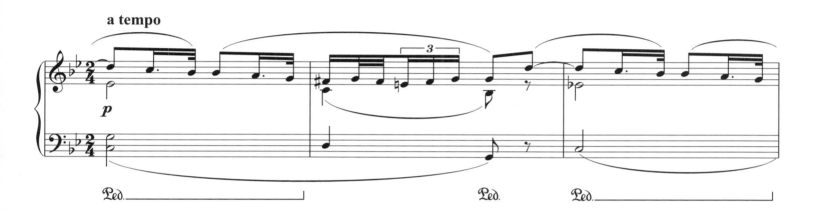

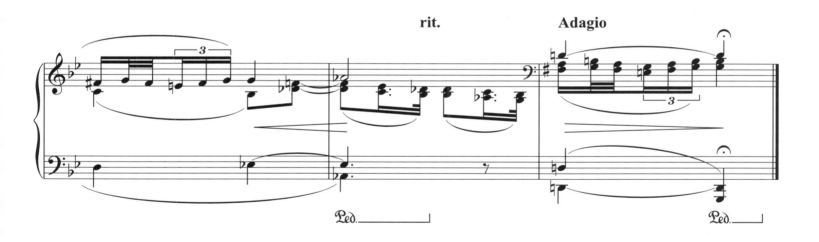

Piece No.1

from Night Pieces, Op.23

Composed by Robert Schumann

Rather slow, often restrained ♩ = 100

56

From Foreign Lands And People

from Scenes From Childhood, Op.15

Composed by Robert Schumann

Child Falling Asleep
from Scenes From Childhood, Op.15
Composed by Robert Schumann

* Orig.

Theme With Variations

from Sonatas For The Young, Op.118

Composed by Robert Schumann

Sonata For Children, Op.118, No.1
(1st Movement)

Composed by Robert Schumann

Theme in E♭ Major

Composed by Robert Schumann

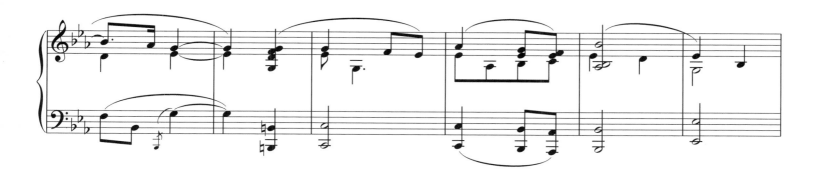

Träumerei

from Scenes From Childhood, Op.15

Composed by Robert Schumann

An Die Sterne
(To The Stars)

Composed by Robert Schumann   Arranged by Quentin Thomas

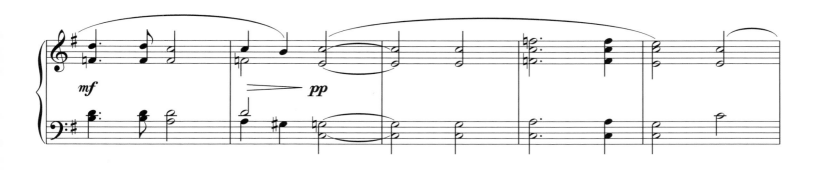

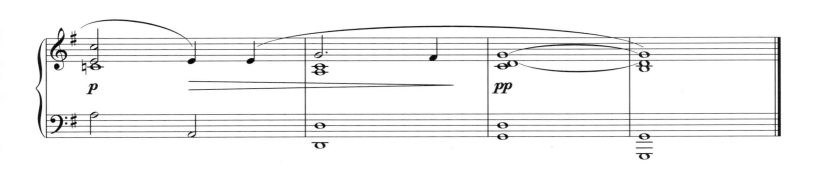

Widmung
(Wedding Dedication)
from Myrthen, Op.25

Composed by Robert Schumann   Arranged by Quentin Thomas

Langsam

rit.   a tempo

Du Bist Wie Eine Blume
(Sweet As Any Flower)

from Myrthen, Op.25

Composed by Robert Schumann   Arranged by Quentin Thomas

Stille Thränen
(Hidden Tears)
from 12 Gedichte, Op.35

Composed by Robert Schumann   Arranged by Quentin Thomas

Sehr langsam

a tempo

rit.

rit.   **Adagio**

78

Ich Will Meine Seele Tauchen

(I Will Immerse My Soul)

from Dichterliebe, Op.48

Composed by Robert Schumann   Arranged by Quentin Thomas

Frei

mit ped.

rit.

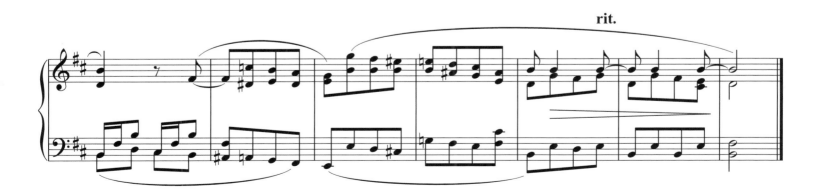

Ich Grolle Nicht
(I'm Not Grumbling)
from Dichterliebe, Op.48

Composed by Robert Schumann   Arranged by Quentin Thomas

Nicht schnell

Im Wunderschönen Monat Mai
(In The Wonderful Month Of May)

from Dichterliebe, Op.48

Composed by Robert Schumann   Arranged by Quentin Thomas

rit.

Er Und Sie
(Him And Her)

Composed by Robert Schumann   Arranged by Quentin Thomas

allargando   a tempo

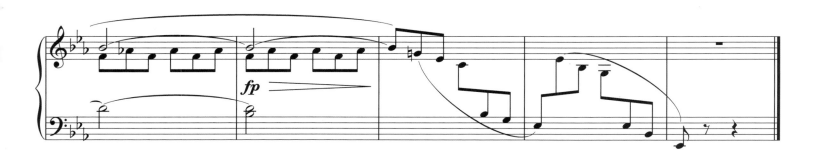

String Quartet in A Major, Op.41, No.3

(2nd Movement: Un poco adagio)

Composed by Robert Schumann   Arranged by Quentin Thomas

cresc.

dim.

un poco rit.

89

Piano Quartet in E♭ Major, Op.47

(3rd Movement: Andante cantabile)

Composed by Robert Schumann   Arranged by Quentin Thomas

Andante Cantabile (♩ = 84)

cantabile e poco a poco cresc.

rit.

p

Symphony No.2 in C Major, Op.61

(3rd Movement: Adagio espressivo)

Composed by Robert Schumann   Arranged by Quentin Thomas

Adagio espressivo (♪ = 76)

un poco rit.

a tempo